METAMORPHOSIS

METAMORPHOSIS

Poetry for Writers and Other Creatives

ELI WINFIELD

ArbreRoche Publishing

*This book is dedicated
to you, Dear Reader,
Because
You were called
to create,
to be brave and do the work,
and to have the strength
and courage
to let your Work into the world.*

CONTENTS

Foreword

This collection of poems was written while I was recovering from a
serious concussion and wondering if I would ever really write again.
The poems talk about my life as a writer and many use my art (words
on the page) as images of doing the work of an artist. But the life of an
artist, the struggles of an artist, and all those things (good and bad)
that go with sharing your art with the world—remain the same no
matter what the medium.

You are not alone. We all struggle with fear, with carving out time to
create, with family and friends who don't understand our call, with
letting go, with criticism and worrying about where we fit into
community. Each of these is part of challenge of being called to create
art and let it go into the world.

My hope is that this collection of poems, such a gift from my own
muse, will be a gift to you and help you find the strength and courage
to do the work you are called to do and then let your work go out into
the world.

Eli Winfield, 2019

Writing

W riting is
Dancing naked on the rooftop
Covered in glitter
Raising hands of joy to the sun
Warmth holding you
Caressing you.
Words, movement, joy,
All come from that centre.

SCARS, WARTS, CELLULITE
Are nothing here.
It isn't about the outside
Or the watchers who aren't watching.
It is about the presence gift
Song and words and image and Art,
Flinging itself into the world
Through our hands
Embodied by our work and
Hope from deep within.

. . .

WRITING IS FLINGING ARMS WIDE
    Striving for the spin
    Letting our work
    Becoming Butterflies that
    Leap and flow and drift.
    It is coming from darkness
    and moving to love;
    Being authentic
    and moving to peace;
    About knowing who we are
    Yet still moving to hope.

WRITING IS WORDS ON PAPER,
    Deepest fears, best joys,
    Arms wide to the world.
    Holding ourselves to account
    From that place of presence,
    Taking our space and knowing, creating
    From the Wild Joy moving within us.
    The performance, the dance,
    The art, the song,
    The words on paper.
    Those are what matter.
    When we are there, when we let go,
    When we dance naked on rooftops,
    We are doing our joy.

WRITING IS
    Letting words metamorphose
    Like Butterflies into the world.

Breathe

B reathe into art.
    Let it be embodied—paint,
    Paper, brushes, silence.
A flower, a moment
A practice.

BREATHE INTO MUSIC
    The beauty of the keyboard
    Scales and clashing chords
    Chasing away the silence
    With fragile hope.

BREATHE INTO THE QUIET
    And listen to the rustle
    The wind you cannot see
    The sun you cannot hear
    The wishes you cannot touch
    The love you cannot hold

Cannot quantify or measure.

BREATHE
Into beauty and mess and hope
Let the drips be as much
A part of your art
As the finished beauty of the flower
On the canvas.

BREATHE.

Rainbows of Hope

W hy do I write?

I WRITE BECAUSE IT IS PART OF ME
    Part of what pulls me
    Out of myself
    Into the bigger space of the world.
    It makes me feel less alone.
    Less afraid.
    Acknowledges that I am broken
    But beautiful too.
    Words run through my pen
    Like sunshine through broken glass
    Shedding rainbows around me.

I WRITE BECAUSE WORDS ARE MY PAINTINGS
    Beauty from a vision in my mind
    On a sea of white space

Colours exploding across
The sky of imagination with the
Black of the ink
Magic that flows through me.
Words like canoes
across the islands of solitude
Carrying hope and dreams
Supplies
Against alone.

I WRITE TO CULTIVATE ORDER IN THE WILD
Not straight path gardens
of formal symmetry
But a space to pass through the
Deep wood jungles
Where the orchids bloom
And jaguars hunt the unwary.
Words etching beauty onto the jagged rocks
Beside waterfalls roaring in falling tumbles
And gurgling
on the flat shallows of granite
With the steady slow slide.
Water lapping at my ankles
in cool, cold silence
Beside fragrant pines
and whispering poplars.

I WRITE AS WITNESS.
Witness to the beauty of life
And the destruction,
The joy that soars
And the despair that drowns,
Those things we have created
which make us great

And those which pull the world around us
Into chaos
Into blackness
Into death.

I WRITE
So my words may become
Rainbows of Hope
shining through the broken glass of life
Black words on white paper
Never knowing
What colour will fill my page.

Become

little at a time,
   One step in front of the other,
   Become.

You can do this.
   Even when you are afraid you are not
   good enough to climb the mountain.
   Trust the guide.
   Just put one step in front of the other.
   Make the goals little steps
   Moving you forward
   Finding a life of hope, of courage, of reality.

Reject the put downs.
   They don't live in your head.
   Hold the gift
   The gold coins you were given
   And do what you need to do.

Be who you were intended to be.
Go forward.
Let the worry about THEM go.

JUST BE YOU.
Put your words on the paper.
Hands on keyboard,
Black and white on the imagination.

YOU ARE CALLED TO THIS LIFE.
Fake it until you become it
And walk that mountain.
Take the pose of presence.
Presence in your own skin.
Presence in your own life.

LET THE WRITING GO.
Let it become alive
Beyond the confines of the white paper.
Alive to the reality of other's imaginations.
A dragon's egg of laughter, joy and fame.
Understand that change comes to us all.
Let it go.
Let it change the world.
And just become you.

Butterflies

I choose
    To let the words in
    Swirl onto my mind and heart.
Be written
Pen on paper, clacking keys in darkness,
Rolling onto the visions in my mind
Flow in, flow out again.
Rejoiced in.
Words that are Witness
Butterflies onto the winds
Of this time, this space,
This place.
Standing for truth
Not manipulations of facts and emotions.
Standing for beliefs,
Values, hopes, honesty.

I CHOOSE TO BREATHE INTO THAT CONNECTION
    To the Hold Joy that is other

Outside me, yet inside me.
I choose to hold that connection here.
Deep calm, Focused Silence
Breath in,
Move pen, life, heart
And then, to breathe out
into the world.

I CHOOSE
　　To let myself stand in this moment.
　　I am not naked on the rooftop.
　　I am clothed in that joy
　　That hope, that connection.
　　And my life, my words,
　　Are those butterflies
　　Testaments to what I stand for
　　What I long for in my deepest heart.

I AM NOT ALONE IN THESE.
　　I am one of the many
　　Called to witness
　　To pen words into the silence
　　To be prophet
　　Voices of calling
　　Speaking words, writing words
　　That fly into the world
　　And echo the deepest heart in all of us.

Joy

Today, in spite of the chaos around me
I choose Joy.
Joy is not happiness or perfection
or safety.
Joy is not laughter
Or always smiling.
Joy is a deep abiding hope
That makes me more aware of my blessings.
Even during the blackest moments of my life.
Because Joy is not dependent
on emotion
On circumstances
On things being Perfect.
Joy is a choice.

Joy is the choice to ask questions
To find the good
To seek awareness
To step forward.

To walk up the mountain
Out of the pit of frustration
Self blame, hurt,
Depression, anger, despair,
No matter what happens
What has happened.
To do my best, to let go of the rest.
To own my struggles
And then put down the worries
That belong to things I do not, cannot control.

JOY IS A CHOICE
To turn to the beautiful
The caring, the real, the positive.
To contemplate the good,
So all of these live in me.
To speak justice and truth
Knowing it might not be popular
But this is my call.
I will follow my own path
Even when it is hard,
Disagree even when it makes me look weird.
Joy is not weak or wimpy.
It is strength and grace in the face
Of opposition
Of challenge
Of pain and hurt and anger.

TODAY
I choose.
I choose Joy.

Snapshots

S it at your desk, pen in hand
And capture the moments of your life.
Words on paper are your camera.

Laughing outside
Running through the ice cold sprinkler
Pony tails flying
The baby toddling behind
A grubby wooden train in her hand
While the dog yips
And dances back and forth
Just out of reach of the artificial rain.

The lights on the Christmas tree
Filling the empty room with hope
Spreading its branches across the centuries
A place to play out stories
Of space invaders

And worlds yet unknown.

THE NIP OF THE COLD AGAINST THE VERDANT GREEN
    Of lush summer grass
    The gentle patter of rain
    A scatter of grey on the silent silver of the the lake
    While you sit and watch
    Grey clouds roll over whistling poplars.

EACH MOMENT IS A PHOTOGRAPH
    A memory captured
    By the scratch of the pen on paper.
    Words painting pictures
    On the screens of your imagination.

SIT AT YOUR DESK
    Pen in hand.
    Capture the moment.
    Words are your Camera.

Morning Musings

One more step on the road
　　A willingness to love,
　　To write,
To put words onto paper
No matter the outcomes
Understanding that I am a writer.
I am open to joy, to becoming
To channelling those words,
Images, scenes, stories
Each of them practical love.

Pen to paper, stories to the world.
　　A moment of calm intention
　　While the coffee perks in the background
　　And the world holds its breath
　　A pregnant pause of silence
　　While my family dreams.

. . .

MY DREAMS ARE BLACK ON WHITE
    Penned in sweeping strokes
    In quiet manifestation.
    Love and despair,
    Hope and sorrow
    Joy and loneness,
    Gliding across the papers
    As I let the words become manifest
    Through my hands.

SOMETIMES MY WORDS
    Don't meet the mark.
    They are like a small child,
    Beloved but not quite right.
    But sometimes!
    Sometimes the words on the page
    Glow with a power
    Beyond anything I can image
    And carry with them a wild joy
    And I read them later in awe.
    I am only the messenger.

I SIP MY COFFEE,
    Listen to the silence
    Where words run across my mind
    A symphony no one else can hear
    Until I pen it in words.
    Today I sit in silence.
    Today I choose to write.

Practice

When I am honest
  I can admit to myself
  I yearn to be a writer,
To write words that are widely read
To be someone celebrated, feted,
Invited to speak to others
About writing,
About facing
Their lives, their fears, their dreams
About overcoming challenges
While still making art.

BUT I STRUGGLE
  To make room
  To do this work of mine
  In my everyday life.
  I struggle to let go
  To let my art have life
  Outside me.

. . .

So,
    Just for today,
    I will focus on one tiny step.
    Not on the big picture—no—
    That is a terrifying pit of unknown—
    But on removing one tiny chip
    Off the marble monument
    Of my writing life.
    I will focus on writing
    Just one word on the page
    In front of me.

Today
    I will focus on motion,
    On Flailing forward and
    Moving myself towards my dreams.
    Inspire myself towards becoming
    That person who dreams inside me.
    Today I will trust that Wild Joy
    Allow it to use my pen to
    Paint breath taking stories
    With words on paper
    Making connections between us.

Today, I will get myself out of the way
    Do my job,
    Put pen to paper.
    Just this next step.
    Just this next moment.
    Just this next word.

Sunrise

R ise to dawn.
        Find the centre,
        the deep hidden heart
And hold to it.
Hope and joy
Despair and pain.
Face the sun
Words on paper.
Each morning is a gift.
Procrastination is not a good tool
To avoid the night.

RISE TO THE NEW DAY
    Face the warmth and
    Accept the vulnerable broken
    The hopeful and the sad
    The panic that freezes your bones
    And the wild laughter
    That makes you dance.

Turn your face to the
Weak rays that slowly
Light the horizon and
Call you to see deep into the shadows
And bring those parts of you
Darkest shame, deepest sorrow,
Into the light.
Broken but beloved.

RISE TO THE NEW DAY
Knowing you are
Battered and bloody.
Clean your wounds.
Wash the blood away,
Bind them again when they are dry.
They itch as they heal,
Uncomfortable,
But that discomfort is part of the healing.
You are not the same today
As you were before the battle.
Your face is scarred
But still you rise,
Put pen to paper,
Write.

RISE TO THE NEW DAY,
Put pen to paper.
By facing the dawn
You are hope.

One

One thing at a time.
One day at a time.
Focus on the now,
On the can,
On the 'am able to'
Instead of the black cloud of
Loss and despair.

One moment.
One breath.
Each a blessing.
None are promised.
So sit.
Sit and breathe.
Sit and become.

Breathe in love,
Light and laughter.

Hold it in your heart
Swirl it in your gut
And let it out again.
Words on paper.
One moment, one hope,
One breath,
One word at a time,
One.

Deep Water

Become deep water
  always striving
    Wild against the rocks of circumstance
But write where you are.
Accept that each piece you write
Is a another stepping stone,
A marker along the path.
Let them fall like rain
Be scattered like feathers in the wind
A painting of beauty, of hope,
Of despair and sorrow and change
Across the landscape of your life.

Write where you are now, knowing
  Where you are now is not
  Who you were yesterday
  And not what you will become tomorrow.
  Commit to the practice

And let the words fall onto the paper.
Each moment penning words to paper
A strengthening of the connection
To that Wild Joy.
Let there be many connections, many paths made
So that your heart has the path to shine
Onto the paper and out into the world.
Hold that wild joy high
And fling it into the abyss of darkness
A candle, a flame of hope in the despair of the world.

When the water rises,
    When struggles come and the words are hard,
    Hold to the river.
    Hold to the steady dip of the paddle
    Pulling against the raging water.
    Keep paddling
    One word at a time,
    One piece at a time.
    One practice for today.
    But many such practices over a lifetime,
    Many pieces of broken pebbles, glass, and words.

Scatter the pieces of glass across the surface of the river.
    Let them be polished in the rushing stream.
    Sink into the rhythm of the padding
    The water, the river, the moment.
    Words on paper are ripples
    Against the waters of time.
    Moments of
    Letting go
    Pushing forward with
    Deep steady strokes

Against the story.

THE WORDS, THE WRITING, THE ART,
    That is your gift.

Pick Up Your Pen

L ife matters.
      Hope matters.
      Your words matter
So write.
Do not allow yourself
To become distracted
By foolish things.
Don't be deceived
Or kept from your work
By criticism or fear.
Stay strong.
Pick up your pen
And write.

Hands on Keyboard

Writing depth.
    Writing tears.
    Writing hope into darkness,
Rainbows into the rain.

FINDING BEAUTY.
    Clinging to it even
    When it feels like dawn will never come.
    Here
    Here is joy.
    Here is the hope of tomorrow.
    Here is truth.

LET THE LIES BE LIES.
    Reject them.
    Turn to love,
    To creation, to belief.
    Turn to the wild joy.

Reject the evil that kills your soul
The lies that whisper
You are 'not good enough'
Or 'you do not have enough time'
Or 'good enough words..

LET THE GREEN OF LIFE
Slither through the cracks
Onto the page
And cling to life
Embodied in those stolen moments.
Let the joy, the tears, the fear
Become black and white.
Let them go
Words on the page.
Do your work.
Put your
Hands on keyboard,
Heart in gear,
Your work is black and white words
Dreams breaking open the darkness.

Practice

Millions of words of practice
flow on the pages
A testament of joy
Of hope
Of becoming
Looking past that dim light
Into that dirty mirror
To the heart in each of us.
Story gifted, shared
Revealed,
Revered
Then carried on the wings of a butterfly
Out into the world.
Fluttering silently, never pausing
Or yelling in the square
Like a prophet of old.
Use your words carefully.
They are the swords of truth.
Long after you have put them down
Stuffed them into a dusty drawer

The smell of musty dust paper
In some old box
They testify to something
Beyond this moment
Called to be free
Out into the world like
Crystallized dreams of hope.

Damocles Sword

S o many hopes and dreams abandoned
      Broken by the threat of Damocles Sword,
      That ever present spectre of death,
Yet I choose
To continue walking on moss covered slopes
Under the spreading arms of the great oaks
Beside calm waters.

I CHOOSE TO LOVE, TO BREATHE
    To bind myself to hope and life.

I CHOOSE TO BECOME,
    To step into the light
    Instead of hiding myself
    In the shadows
    A chipped and dancing stone giantess
    Raising crowned head to the sun
    To take up the dance in the meadow

Hoping there will be someone to join me,
That I will not always feel alone
And alien.

Is it my skin, my form, that separates?
 Or is it my unwillingness to share
 This giant hope
 This calling voice
 That shifts inside me?
 That calls me to dance out loud in joy?

So today,
 Just today,
 I nod to the sword,
 Step to the edge of the forest
 And raise my arms
 To feel the sun.

Stress

Acknowledge the stress.
Let it be there like
Sunset colours painted on the sky.

THEN LET IT GO.
Let it Fade
Like ashes carried away on the wind
Not bottled up in your heart.
Memories held in love
Faced with courage
Real for but a moment and then
Let go
in breath and calm.
Tied to balloons like prayers on the wind.

BE REAL.
Be present.
Write.

Morning Pages

L ost my glasses.
No morning pages until
I can see.

Fail Forward

Don't worry about winning
    About sprinting to the gold.
    This is a marathon.
The goal is to cross the finish line
To run a good race,
To make connections,
To grow,
To write to the end.

Don't worry about good enough.
    Do your best.
    Ask questions,
    Become.
    Write.

Believe in the story.
    Write what the story needs
    And enjoy the process.

Spend your time,
The quantity you cannot edit back.

LET YOURSELF FAIL FORWARD
So you begin to
Fall in the direction you want to be going.
Be yourself, gracious and caring,
Outside the middle
Dealing with the fringes
And be Ok with it.
Write.

Dealing with Dragons

My muse whispers
    Keep it real.
    Keep it between the lines—
Between the moments.
Between breaths.
Let it go.
Stress only hurts you.
It doesn't change the moment.

So I pull up my socks
    Take a breath
    Face the space and time.
    Long range plans
    Short range plans
    Write it out
    Grateful I can
    Grateful I am still able to put words on paper.
    Because for a while
    That wasn't on the list of my can-dos.

. . .

So, EVEN THOUGH MY HEAD HURTS WHEN I WRITE
    Even though it is harder
    And I still have days when I go home
    And crash in a chair
    Stumble into bed
    A shadow of the former me
    Different
    I know I am becoming.

I HOLD TO HOPE,
    Believing there are possibilities
    That this week things will improve
    That this month will be different
    That I will be able
    Eventually.
    Always Eventually.

THERE IS THAT MOMENT IN BETWEEN
    When I am looking at myself in the mirror,
    Stuck between where I am and who I am becoming.
    I look out.
    I am alone again,
    Alone in my head with the headphones
    Alone in the space with the silence
    Alone with hopes for the dreams
    Of words on the paper.
    Alone between the heart beats
    Alone with dragons.

Perfect

Perfect stops me dead,
Keeps me from trying,
Keeps me frozen in fear.

So I sidestep.
Try to deal with the concrete:
A character sketch, a map,
The grocery list,
The dishes, the floors, the laundry
Anything but the fear.

Slowly I step around the yawning chasm,
Breathe,
Then slide onto more solid ground.
I let the words run on paper
A vomit of wishes
Desperate emotions
And misspelled broken sentences

Scribbled in darkness.

IDEAS CLINGING TO REALITY
Between crossed off words.
I hope something there
Is worth reading.
My heart wishes for easy and smooth
But the path is jagged and lonely.

I STOP.
Admire the view for a moment,
And begin the climb again.
One word at a time
Clinging to the paper.
And when my heart weeps
I remember the view.

Rainbows in the Rain

Hands on keyboard,
   Writing depth, writing tears,
   Writing hope into the darkness and
Rainbows into the rain.
Finding beauty and clinging to it
Even when it feels dawn will never come.
Letting go and knowing:
Here is joy.
Here is the hope of tomorrow.
Here is truth.

Reject the evil that kills your soul
   That tells you the lies
   Like you are 'not good enough'
   'You don't have enough time'
   'You don't have enough words'.
   Turn your back on the lies and
   Put your hands on the keyboard.

                    . . .

TURN TO LOVE, TO CREATION, TO BELIEF.
    Let the green of that Wild Joy
    Slither through the cracks of your time
    Onto the page and cling to life
    Embodied in those stolen moment
    Black words on white paper.

LET THE JOY, THE TEARS,
    The fear, the hope,
    Become the black and white whispers
    That changes the world,
    Become words.
    Words that grow dreams, tell stories,
    Call the flames of the imagination.

LET THE FEARS GO.
    Do your work:
    Hands on keyboard,
    Heart in gear,
    Words on the page
    Rainbows through broken glass
    Shining joy into the world.

Face Yourself

Face yourself.
Let yourself be that crazy, fun, joyous wonder
Who laughs,
Who loves,
Who mucks in the mud
And makes friends with the neighbours,
Who fills your world with flowers
And the smell of lemon oil
And the joy of space.

Make space to create,
to dance, to laugh,
to explore
To paint beautiful pictures
Words on the page
Paint on the canvas,
The fabric between the pins,
The art in your mind
And under your fingers.

. . .

MAKE SPACE TO STRETCH OUT YOUR ARMS IN THE SUNLIGHT
Feel the wood under your feet,
The sand between your toes,
The deep dark earth staining your legs,
Your hands,
Ink on your nose and the smell of the wild woods
Vivid in your mind
As you stir the soup on the stove.

Real

Real is my eyes twitching
       And the print blurring.
       Real is eating again
To control the nausea.
Real is waking up my child
To go to work
Putting on the kettle
To say I love you.
Real is carrying on
after taking three extra strength Tylenol.
Real is picking up after yourself.

REAL IS LETTING THINGS
    That used to be quick and easy
    Become deliberate and plodding
    And then turning around
    And putting the frustration into fiction,
    Letting it play out
    Romping across the paper.

. . .

REAL IS LEARNING TO ACCEPT THAT
    Different isn't bad
    Even when you want
    To scream with frustration and pain
    Like a two year old
    Who dropped her ice cream.
    Real is choosing to smile
    Because training your brain to be present
    Is part of the process.

REAL IS KNOWING THERE WILL BE BAD DAYS
    But they won't last.
    You just have to keep walking
    Keep laughing
    Keep trying.
    Keep accepting life will change.
    Real is knowing energy is finite
    And so is time.

REAL IS PUTTING
    Words on the paper
    One after the other.
    Taking only this moment.
    Breathe. Become.
    Allow. Acknowledge.
    Feel the space, the emotions.
    Pen the words.
    Breathe through it.
    Let go.
    Become Real.

Today

Today I thinned out my shoes and my purses.
        Tidied my space
        And then I walked away,
Took a breath
And sat down to write.
Not always an easy choice
or an obvious benefit.

TODAY I CHOSE
    To fall in love with the process
    To enjoy the boring
    mucky middle
    The painful staggering through
    And put words on paper.

TODAY
    I chose to set beauty with life and heart
    Into words and let them go.

My words are just one tiny twinkling star
against the galaxy of
Wide and beautiful skies
Painted across paper.
Just one of the many
worlds still to be imagined.

Less

I stare at the pictures,
   Click like,
   Move on.
Images of a Perfect life:
Tidy house,
Well fed children,
Sex body,
Rich prayer life,
Five best friends,
Perfectly prepared
Four course meals,
Fourteen books released,
All best sellers.

In that moment of moving on
   I wilt.
   The perfect in my mind is overwhelming.
   My life is messy.
   It doesn't fit neatly into those little pretty images,

doesn't summarize to one hundred and forty four characters.
But it is full, too,
Full of life and music and colour, wild connections.

FEELINGS OVERWHELM ME.
My home overwhelms me.
So many pieces everywhere.
Who am I called to become
While I am climbing this mountain?

LESS IS HARD.
Tidy is the space defining my openness
To growth, to change.
Have I chosen to barricade myself into the mess
To hold the world at bay
To hide from my fear of sharing my gifts in the world?
Because there is too much:
Too much judgement
Too much picture perfect
Too much terrifying possibility,
Too much hope in the wild and open spaces?

CAN I TAKE ONE SMALL TINY STEP AND
Let go of one small thing?
Materials for a project no longer relevant,
Boxes and bags no longer needed?
Can I forgive myself the many unused things
Buffering my world with clutter?
Can I allow myself to open one small window of space?
Can I let go of words,
Put them on paper?

. . .

I FIND LESS
    One moment at a time,
    One step at a time.
    Set an intention
    Move in a positive direction
    Open myself to the wild joy,
    To the Real
    That changes everyone.

REAL MATTERS.
    I listen to my pain, hold it close
    Enfold it in angel wings of accepting love.
    Remind myself:
    I am loved as I am.
    I am valued as I am.
    I open myself to the world
    And share my words,
    Breathe into the space
    And realize
    I AM NOT ALONE.

Slow Death by Domesticity

Innovation.
    See things in a new way.
    Believe in that big magic outside you
The connection between us all
The gift that comes through us and
Changes us.
Rise with the sun.
Take a moment.
Ready your tools
Then let yourself.
Let yourself dream.
Let yourself write.

It won't be perfect
    But you will hear it.
    It won't be easy
    But the dreams are vivid
    Verdant romps of words against
    A sky of gold

In the early morning light.
I miss the dreams
When I join the real world.

AFTERNOON.
    Evening.
    Not the same.
    The dreams are pale reflections.
    My mind is full of the day's emotions
    Disappointments
    Dramas.
    The pen sits silent
    And the house nags in the background.

DON'T DREAM.
    Don't write.
    Pick up the mess.
    Clean the sink.
    Wash the tub
    With a toothbrush.

SLOW DEATH BY DOMESTICITY
    While the wild greens
    Beckon from afar
    And dragons soar
    On words unwritten.

Make Space

Make space
    For me
    For my dreams
And the dreams of my family
So that their hands can create
The beauty in their minds.

MAKE SPACE TO BREATHE
    To become open to the world.
    To family visiting with no notice
    To friends staying when they need to
    To hope becoming embodied by love
    And practicality.

IT ISN'T ABOUT PICTURE PERFECT
    About magazine spreads
    Or vision boards.
    It is about the experience

Living a full and rich life
Creating
And letting go.

IT IS ABOUT BEING WELCOMING
In the moment
And knowing love
Wins hope
Creates friendship and caring.

IT IS ABOUT HAVING TEA TOGETHER
Sweeping sawdust from the corners
And sitting by the fireplace with a book.
It is about joy in the day
Being settled with hope
About acknowledging the blessings
You have been given
And sharing them with others.

IT IS ABOUT LETTING GO
Of expectations that keep you
From knowing hope
From knowing laughter
From knowing love
Because you are stuck on should,
On the piles buffering you from life.

SO TAKE A MOMENT,
Breathe,
And then let go.

. . .

Breathe into the space between the piles.
Breathe into the hope of your calling.
Breathe into the quiet between the lines,
The ink on your pen and words on the page.

Then take courage
And carve out more for yourself.
Carve away the excess, the overwhelm.
Let go of the guilt and the should.
Carve into the piles
Until you reveal the gift of you
Of all you love
Of all you believe in
Of all you value.
Let those things that no longer serve you
Fly to become
Blessings to other.

Carve out space
To let yourself create.

Revision

I stare at the pile of pages on my desk.
It is ok, I tell my self.
It is just a first draft.
It is Ok,
Ok to let things need work,
Need editing
Need changes.

HOLDING THIS DRAFT IS LIKE STARING AT
A marble chunk
That holds the beautiful angel
With unfurled wings and flowing hair
And struggling to chip away at the rock
Chip, chip, chip,
Trying to carve away the unnecessary
So that the beauty
Can be admired by the world.

. . .

REVISION IS DAUNTING.

I TELL MYSELF
    One day at a time,
    One word at a time.
    Let myself struggle with
    Story logic, story beats, story hope.
    Let it be. Let it become.

SOME DAYS THERE ARE
    3 pages in the rain of my self doubt
    And I cannot face the pile of pages.
    I go back to long hand,
    A different dream,
    A different story
    Letting my words fall like raindrops in a thunderstorm,
    Letting the muse romp across the page in the depths
    Poetry and prose
    hope and struggle.
    I let it all fall onto the white page
    A river of scribbles and struggle,
    Allow myself to put down the wrong words.

THEN I THINK ABOUT WRITING
    About becoming an author with published books.
    About editing my words and
    The fears rise.
    What if I flop?
    What if my husband leaves me?
    What if my friends laugh?
    What if it is horrible?
    Or what if it is really good
    And people hate it when I get better?

. . .

IN THE SILENT CONDEMNATION OF SELF DOUBT
Whispered hope speaks, holds me up.
Let it be.
Let it go.
Do your work.
Let your art become
Blessing into the world.
Let there be words on the page,
A deep meaning of joy and laughter and challenge.

BUT HOW DO I DO THAT?
How do I find that creative supportive place?
Will I ever find
Those angels with human hands
Voices of calm and hope
In the chaos of life
When the words are dark
And I cannot find my way?

I SEARCH FOR THE FOOTHOLDS ON THE ROCKS
The narrow paths of joy
Carved by others who climbed this mountain.
There are others on this journey
Lifting me up
Encouraging me to the next rock, the next step.
They give me the strength to let them help me
And from somewhere deep inside me
I find the strength to help others
Crawling behind me on the path.

I WANT TO SEE THE VISTA AT THE TOP OF THE MOUNTAIN

To see the hills, feel the wind move my hair.
I want to live,
To give others a hope, a belief, a vision.
I want to make my mark in the world.
To leave art
Words, pictures, poems,
Stories that matter.
Deep abiding story.

I FACE THE FEARS
Pick up my red pen
Stare at the scribbles on the page.
And begin my revision once more
Carving out my vision of joy
One painful word at a time.

Wings

When I was young
    Stories were words on the page
    Carried on the winds of my imagination.
When did I let them have weight?
Tie them down to keep them safe.

It is time to give them wings
    Let them off the Chains
    Butterflies into the world
    Content to fly.

Reframe

Stop.
    Reframe the fear:
    This is excitement.
Count down five to one
And then
Go!
Out into the next space.
Make a plan.
Troubleshoot
But don't stop.
It is about light,
Movement,
Hope.
The next hope.
The next words.
Listen.
Love.
Believe.
Let go.

Sailing

Do not fear beginning
Or pausing on the road to recharge.
Fear stopping.
Fear losing hope.
Fear knowing you lost a chance
Stopped in a port for provisions
And didn't try again.
Fear failure for failure's sake,
Not for what you learned.

Take heart.
There are bumps on the road,
Rocky storms that drive you off course
And break your hope
With gaping holes of self doubt,
Fissures and cracks in the boat of your hope
Broken wings against the sky.
Yet each rocky moment,
Each wild storm, brings with it

A chance to change course,
A chance to rise.

TODAY YOU ARE NEW.
Let yourself be reborn.
You cannot change yesterday,
The choices that brought you into the port,
The broken hull, the tattered sails.
The desperate wishes of tomorrow
Are dust on the mirror
Of the choices that set you on this path.
Brush them away so you can see now.
Focus on today.

TODAY YOU CAN CHANGE COURSE.
Today your choices can steer you
Into a new wind with
Small steps
Small course adjustments
That might take you on
A longer voyage.
Rise with the red sun of dawn.
Face the day.
The storm has passed.
Repair the sails,
Take stock of the provisions,
Patch the hull.
But today
Choose to set sail.

Metamorphosis

I want to be OK.
    I am not and it is hard.
    I get better little pieces at a time.
And it is slow.

I INCH MY WAY FORWARD
    Belly crawl through the mud in the cold
    Not knowing where I will end up
    But knowing if I stop here
    If I let myself give up now,
    I will die.

THIS IS NOT THE HILL I WANT TO DIE ON.

SO I CONTINUE
    Putting words on paper,
    Inch forward awkwardly

Knowing my words aren't graceful or smooth
When I get to the other side
I don't know what I will be like.
I will be transformed, changed,
Broken and remade,
Reborn into a life I no longer know.
Hope burns in me
that maybe,
just maybe,
When I am done changing
I will fly.

The Slow Deep Paddle

The long slow deep paddle
Battles with the cacophony of the world.
What do I want?
What do I stand for?

Words swirl around my imagination
Like butterflies.
I struggle to put pen to paper,
To set the words free.
It never seems enough.
The chorus drowns out the small voice
In my heart.
Find Connections, be real, be relevant,
Be loud, ship it out, daily.
I am the canoe stuck on the edge of the river
Watching the raging waters rush past
Wondering if there is a place for me here.
But I stop, listen to my own voice

My own heart.
I let the stress, the fear
Slide away, find my centre.
What do I stand for?
What do I want?

I CHOOSE TO PUT MY PADDLE INTO THE WATER,
When I stand in my centre
I can create
And I can let go of my words
Let them go out into the world
And become more.
Not without fear
But without self judgement
Because I have done the work
Done my best
And that
Is Enough.

WHAT DO I WANT?
It isn't enough to say I want to make money,
Be on panels
Speak about writing, about creating,
About listening to those voices within
And living an authentic life of creating.
I want to go all over the world
Sharing my art
Sharing my words.
Knowing that others may not love them
But not letting that stop me.
I want to know I made a difference
To my children, to my love,
To my friends and colleagues,

To my readers.
I want to be ok with my words
Making ripples
Changing the world around me.

I WANT TO WRITE.

Hidden Dreams

So many stories to let go of
Hiding in a drawer.
So many moments of joy and fear
And love.
Believe in my dream,
Broken and whole
Imperfect yet able
Striving to become.
Learn, teach, do.
Always do.

OPEN THE DRAWER,
Blow away the dust of fears.
Polish the words.
Then have the courage
To let those hidden dreams go
To touch the imaginations of others.
Let them become joy and laughter
And hope in the light.

Torrent

Let the torrent flow past
    Then let it go.
    Let things become calm.
I choose to create my art
My sense of beauty, of blessing
Words thrown into the world.
I give myself permission
To have struggles
To have fears and hurts
But still be ok.

DID I CAUSE THIS CHAOS?
    Is this guilt mine to carry.
    I am gifted and broken,
    Whole and struggling.
    I need to bleed off the poison of
    Anger and injustice,
    Of blame for failure.

The truth is heavy.
I hear the words and repeat them:
You are resilient
Smart and capable.
You will figure it out.

Deep Quiet Real

Deep quiet real.
>The space between the lines
>Between the words.
The moments of hope and joy
Where love shines
Even through my broken
Struggling words.

DEEP QUIET REAL
That reacts to attacks
Not with anger or retaliation
But with dignity
And an eye to the goal.

DEEP QUIET REAL
Standing on the rock
Not the shifting sands of fate

Climbing the mountain
With Joy in your hands
And words on the page.

Deep quiet real.

Serenity

Q uiet sitting, trying to
    Breathe serenity into stress.
    Watch thoughts pass
    Like stinging hornets on a rampage.
Breathe into the belly
Count the measured slow
Deep breaths
While the storm rages.
Remember
Above the clouds
The sun still shines.

HOLD THE HURT.
    Cradle it but know
    You are separate from it.
    Like a child full of anger and fury, it will calm.
    All it needs is that moment of open
    Of acceptance.
    Choose

Not to push it away
Not to deny its existence
But not to act blindly on it either,
Or allow it to run the show like a spoiled toddler.
Just to hold it, accept it and then, let it pass.

YOU ARE NOT THE SORROW, THE PANIC, THE MOURNING,
The black cloud of depression.
You are not the bad review.
Not the broken in your life,
the blame or the anger,
The frustration or the hurt.
You are the mountain.
A core of strength, of calm,
With roots that run deeper than you understand
Or know
Into the deep core of this Wild that holds us all.

THE SUN SHINES ABOVE THE STORM,
Seeks to warm you through the dark clouds.
Let the rain fall, bear the hurt away.
Let the pain be carried away
By suddenly rising rivers
And washed clean in deep puddles.
Then
Pick up the pieces.
Sit in calm and take
Slow deep breaths.
Just sit in calm.
Just breathe
Serenity.

Affirmations

S it in silence
	and picture success.
	Affirmations
Are like beads on a prayer string
Believe in your words.
Knowing that
even as you share
Success is a gift
Not a right.

Visualize your life
	As it will be
	Moment by moment
	Blessings heaped onto your plate
	And allow that to become.
	Words into the world
	Like butterflies.

. . .

Sit in silence
    And then the Big Wild Joy that is
    Work in you
    Work through you.

Become.

Become

A little at a time
    One step in front of the other.
    You can do this
Even when you are afraid
You might not be good enough
To climb the mountain
Trust the Muse and the pen.
Make your goals little steps
Movig you forward
To a life of hope,
Of courage, of reality.

REJECT THE PUT DOWNS.
    Instead hold the gift
    The gold coins of story you were given
    And do what you need to do.
    Go forward.
    Let the worry about THEM go.
    Just be you. Do your work.

Put your words on the paper,
Hands on keyboard,
Black and white on the screen
Of your imagination.

YOU ARE CALLED TO THIS LIFE,
    To walk this mountain.
    Take the pose of presence
    Presence in your own skin
    Presence in your own Life
    And become into the life
    You have been given.
    Let the writing go.
    Let it become embodied beyond the confines
    Of the empty page
    Alive to the reality of other's imaginations
    A dragon's egg of laughter, joy and story.
    Let it go.
    Let it change the world.

Wild Joy

Pithy joyous words on the page.
        The magic flows through me
        Lights my imagination,
Shows love
Even to my shadow side,
Beyond jealousy, hurt,
Unintentional harm.

I CHOOSE TO STAND IN THE LIGHT
        And realize I don't know.
        All I can do is allow that love
        To flow through my pen
        Through my actions
        Through my life
        Always feeling like I am
        Missing the mark
        But striving to believe, to hope
        That my words like butterflies
        Will light someone's life

During their darkest times
So they know they are not alone.

WE ARE BROKEN TOGETHER, EACH
    A holograph of bigger joy.
    So I search for the face of that Wild Joy
    In stranger and friend,
    Hope that my life, my actions,
    My words on the paper
    Helps others to see
    The face of that Wild Joy
    Dancing inside in me.

THAT WILD JOY
    Breaks apart the wall of silence
    That divides us,
    Helps me to hold out a hand even
    When others judge my life as phoney
    When I try to love in practical ways,
    When I say I am a writer.

I AM NOT A ONE SIDED EXPRESSION:
    It is not either Art or Science,
    Math or Language
    That lights my soul.
    I am a renaissance scholar.
    Each of these
    Gives me another way to see
    Deeper into the mystery
    That lights us all.
    We are each whole and broken
    Expressions of that Joy.

                    .   .   .

I POUR OUT WORDS ON PAPER
   Fuelled by coffee, tears,
   Wine and laughter.
   My words are
   Voices in the grey of dawn
   Against the rising tide of darkness
   Trying to divide us
   To make us believe
   Only science has answers,
   That only black or white has truth.
   That love cannot change hearts
   And words on the page
   Cannot change the future.
   My words are tiny butterflies
   In the wind changing the world.

I PICK UP MY PEN.
   My writing is defiance against divisions,
   Black on White
   Bringing worlds of grey
   Alive to the imagination.
   I hope my words will give space
   For the Wild Joy to bring forth
   Rainbows in the Light.

Avoidance

How do I?
How do I find that creative supportive place?
Find those angels with human hands,
Voices of calm and hope
In the chaos of life
When the words are dark
And I cannot find my way?

Help me find the foot holds in the rocks
The narrow paths of joy
Carved by others
who climbed this mountain.
Let there be others on this journey,
Lifting me up
Encouraging me to the next rock
The next step.
Give me the strength to let them help me
And the strength to help others
Behind me on this path.

. . .

I WANT TO SEE THE VISTA AT THE TOP OF THIS MOUNTAIN
    To see the hills, feel the wind move my hair.
    I want to live
    To give others a hope, a belief, a vision.
    I want to make my mark in the world
    To leave art
    Words, pictures, stories.
    Stories that matter
    Deep abiding words of joy.

I LOOK AT THIS DRAFT AND SIGH.
    Then I pick up the red pen,
    Face revision once more,
    One painful word at a time.

Community

Community, the connectedness in
The broken.
We cling to the safety rope
Hold the pole of high standards tightly
And carry each other
Over the chasm.
Each one bearing a load.

TOGETHER WE ARE STRONGER
Together we can do far more
Than we can alone.
As long as we can hold on
Have the strength
to move forward
Stand together,
Walk together,
Hold each other up.

. . .

IT TAKES COURAGE
   To keep walking when my feet
   Hit the edge of the cliffs.
   Takes me choosing to trust
   To have faith they won't stop and
   Drop me into the chasm,
   Won't let me fall.

I CLING TO THE POLE,
   Keep walking forward
   Clench the pole tightly
   When my feet dangle over the yawning black
   Pray I will touch ground again.
   This is only a moment.
   Soon my feet will be on solid ground.

Learning

Learning
  To make it easy
  To make it clear
Let myself walk the path
Step along the ways of change
Of becoming.

LEARNING TO WRITE, TO LET THE DREAMS
  Flow on the page
  To become,
  To allow success
  To become part of life.
  Part of my self image,
  Part of my experience.

LEARNING TO DO MY WORK
  Hands on pen.
  To focus on the words

Not the easy or hard.
The job is to
Get the words written.

LEARNING TO DEVELOP SUPPORT
And reach beyond me
Beyond my little corner
And tune myself to the life
I was intended to live.
To grow rooted and flowering
Where I am planted
And believe I can change the world.
I can create a hope
A belief, an understanding.
I am called here.
This is my time, my place, my job.
My time to give my words to the world.

LEARNING TO TRUST,
To let my muse
Help me develop the hope,
The ability, the questions,
The visions and the call.
And the willingness to have others,
Mentors, friends, fans,
Standing at my side.

Slush Pile Social

I pause at the edge of the crowd
    Inch closer, ever hopeful, ever nervous.
    Can I find my place in this world?
Fear clings to my hope.
My heart pounds but
I manage to open my mouth,
To throw myself into the conversations,
Even as my soul is filled with
Agonizing self conscious whispers and
Paralyzing perfectionism
Again.

DARKNESS FALLS.
    I follow the crowds to raucous parties
    Filled with alcohol and
    Fuelled by boasts and banal chatter.
    Stand against the wall
    Waiting for the pearls of wisdom to fall
    As I listen to the voices of giants

And know that I am not one of these.
I write but I am not an author.
My envy stirs.
I want to have my words noticed
Celebrated, read,
But I am just part of the furniture,
Another attendee wanting to become,
Another hopeful in the crowd of many
In the slush pile.

MY MUSE STIRS,
Shakes its head at my fear.
Reminds me to
Stop. Breathe.
Listen. Write.
Always write.
It isn't about the social.
It is about the words,
Dreams that soar on black and white.

I SIT AGAINST A QUIET WINDOW,
Pen in hand,
Open my notebook and my heart,
Pour my writing out
Like stones onto a pond
Creating ripples that carry
To the edges of dreams.
I watch the crowds
And yearn.
Wonder if here I will find a place,
Find my tribe, my people.
Fear stops me,
Keeps me from asking
All those hard questions,

Keeps me from connecting
Even when the hands are held out.

It takes practice for me to
   Becoming ok with those faltering steps
   And the flailing,
   Time for me to find my rhythm.
   I open myself to one of the quiet ones,
   Smile and say hello,
   Ask a question in a panel,
   And hover in the shadows while others
   Ask questions about things I have never
   Even considered and I learn.
   Sometimes magic happens
   And I can move the conversation
   Deeper into the river of understanding.

Standing in the shadows I hear others speak
   The same fears, the same struggles.
   I am not alone with
   My struggle to let go,
   My paralysis speaking about story to others,
   My struggles to find the muse
   Or put pen to paper,
   My self conscious perfectionism, or
   My struggle to dig out
   The diamond of story in the
   Rubble of the first draft.
   I am normal here.
   It is reassuring to understand
   We all struggle with these fears.

Others smile at me,

Invite me for coffee,
Talk and spend time with me
Let me ask those burning questions
I am afraid to speak in the crowds.
I am one of the many quiet ones,
But now I understand
Even the giants struggle with
The same fears.
I listen to wisdom
And in that quiet Sunday morning time
I am grateful to realize there is room for me
At the slush pile social.

Focus

Today, I choose
    Not to be afraid
    Not of success,
Not of failure,
Not of being wrong,
Not of being right
Not of changing the world.

Focusing on my best.
    And allowing the rest—
    The anxiety, the worry, the questions—
    Drift away
    Carried off by balloons of prayer.
    And focus on what I can change.

I intentionally set boundaries of
    Compassion bordered with self care,
    Let other people deal with their own challenges

Focus on my own.
Kindness is not weakness.
It is not foolish or self-serving.
It is not a condemnation of someone else's lack.
Kindness is a gift I choose.

TODAY I SHALL BE ME.
I will not hide.
I will not lower my voice,
Or hide my words on the paper
Or lessen my abilities.
I will invite others, too, to become more deeply.
I will not let my worry
Keep me from hope.
Today I choose to connect, to be in relationship.

I WILL FACE MY FAILURES,
What I have done and what I have failed to do,
And ask for forgiveness.
I will find ways to grow,
To become a thoughtful careful steward,
To tend to the garden of my life
In joy and honesty.
Through it all, knowing there are
Sunrises, wild and full,
Blooming across the joy of earth.

TODAY, I WILL DO MY WORK,
Put my hands on the keyboard,
Let the words become reality.
Today I will be present
And breathe.

Responsibility

My life is my responsibility.
My decisions are mine.
Today I look at my future
And I choose.
I choose options that move my life
In the direction of my dreams
Options that open to abundance
Blessings that are the mark
of the Wild Holy.

I CHOOSE TO LIVE FULLY,
To dance with exuberance,
To find and focus on joy
Not on happiness, a fleeting emotion,
But on Joy
The eternal understanding
That I am loved
And can be love in the world.

. . .

ELI WINFIELD

I CHOOSE TO OPEN MYSELF TO FRIENDSHIP
    To hope in opportunities.
    to sharing my talents
    To finding mentors
    And maintaining family connections.

I CHOOSE TO SPEND MY TIME
    On the accomplishments that matter to me,
    On the dreams I want:
    Prayer through piano,
    Hope through teaching,
    Words worth telling others.

I OPEN MYSELF TO THE IDEA
    That my words
    That my life
    Makes a difference,
    That I am in this place, this situation,
    For a reason
    That I am chosen, and loved and beloved.
    I choose to believe
    That love can be my gift to the world
    Even when I am broken and struggling
    I choose joy.

I CHOOSE WORDS ON THE PAGE
    Hope embodied in scribbles
    That capture the movies in my mind.
    And I choose,
    I choose,
    To let those images and stories,
    Those shaky words on the page
    Out into the world.

Feathers of blessing
Never to be fully gathered back.
They are the paints of my life
These works of my hands,
Flawed yet beautiful.
I give them to the world
As a sign of love,
A mark of joy.

Listen

Balance and calm.
Fairness and focus.
Manage your time, your goals.
Dig deep for that clear understanding
Of where you stand
What you stand for
Where you are going
And then let the rest go.

You cannot manage the complexity of life
The challenges that face you.
Micromanaging the chaos will drown you.
Stand on the rock.
Focus on consistency, on values.
Choose where you paddle
Based on where you are going.
Be who you are, who you are called to be
And Love Deeply, wildly,
Enthusiastically

That you have been given to Love.
Stand for those values you know are right.

DRAW DEEP INTO YOURSELF THE WILD
    Uninhibited Joy that moves through all things
    And let Them love you, move you,
    Change you.
    Then breathe that love out
    Onto the world.
    Not just the Big World,
    But the little corner that is your life
    The people you meet where you are every day.
    Be as loving and generous to family and friends
    As you are to acquaintances and charity.

BE PRESENT IN THE NOW
    Present in your life
    And present to the discontent that changes you.
    Let others tell you their values
    But walk your own
    Knowing that they may not understand
    Why you are walking a different path.
    Your world, your call, your life.

LISTEN TO THAT VOICE
    Still and small
    Hidden on the whispered wind.
    Be a part of the conversations and connect.
    That voice moving through you calls you to become,
    Calls you to speak, to write, to create
    As witness.
    Calls you to be real.

. . .

REAL CHANGES THINGS.
  Real is deep and loving and terrifying
  To those who want easy
  Who see success as things instead of
  Accomplishments and connections.
  Be real anyway.
  Take the slow, deep paddle
  Onto wild rivers still unknown.

OPEN THE WORLD BEYOND YOUR DOORS
  And let life—messy, chaotic, beautiful—change you
  Connect with you.
  But even as it does
  Remember that still deep calm.
  What do you stand for?
  What do you want out of this?

DEEP AND CALM.
  Present and calms.
  Breathe in the moment
  And be.

The Wild Holy

Consider the whole.
 Consider the gifts
 And work towards joy
Towards beauty
Towards love.
Work out your salvation
Work out your hope.

You are the hands, the feet,
 The hope and the angels of the Wild Holy,
 His and her eyes in the world,
 His and her agents of love,
 Bravery in the face of fear.

You are the hope of the world
 The salt of the earth.
 Salt—the ingredient that creates taste
 That brings out the best in others.

Speak your truths,
But remember, too,
That the Wild Holy loved
In spite of our Broken, our Hurtful,
Our actions.

BE AGENTS OF THAT LOVE TO OTHERS
Not expecting glory
Or payment
Or a front page write up.
Do it because it wells up
From your heart,
Because it overflows
From the love you were given.
Do it because
You can do nothing else.

LET YOUR ACTIONS SPEAK
Faith, Hope, Joy Love
Grounded in Wild Joy.
Carry those hurts around you
Into prayers, into words,`
To be folded into the light of the
Love that speaks through each of us.

BE THE HANDS, THE FEET,
The arms, the ears
Of that Diving Wild Joy.
The ones that carry out a Sweater
When someone trying to convert you
Is cold on the side of the road.

. . .

Love breaks stone.
  Water wears away earth
  Into channels of wild torrent.
  Hope cannot be extinguished
  Even in the dark
  Even in death
  If it comes
  From the Wild Holy.

Plans

Long range plans
Short range plans
How do I know the goal,
Adjust mid course?
How come I always feel like a failure?
Am I addicted to that feeling?
Where did it come from?
A lack of hope?
A joy gone missing?
What is success?

A TIDY HOUSE WITH THINGS USED
And space to be creative
Words let out into the world
On a regular basis
A hope to change the world
An honesty.
Working into the next thing.

. . .

FIVE SHORT SHORT STORIES
    Novella
    Novel
    The shape of things to come
    Words out
    Into the world.

WORDS OUT INTO THE WORLD.

Blessings

Naming my weakness,
    Acknowledging it, learning from it,
    Using the gifts I have.

Moving on. Moving up.
    Moving into becoming.
    Creating beauty with words
    Hope on paper
    Black on white.
    The depths of our space,
    Our soul together.

We are the images of God
    Holographs of the trinity
    Of all things male, female and between
    The rainbow expression of identity
    That is the hope of Spirit
    We are all pieces of that existence

We live, move, have our being
Vibrations of love out of time
Beyond space, beyond ourselves.
Beyond lines and doctrines
Beyond Boundaries
enforced by wars, divisions, limitations.

WE ARE PUT HERE TO BE SERVICE
To be Darling
To be gift.
Each part of the greater whole
Called to be deeply
Express deeply who we are.

PICK UP THE PIECES OF YOUR LOVE,
Life in action,
The gift that you are.
Unwrap it.
Become it.
Write your life on paper
And then let your gift go.
Every piece is
Blessing given to the world.

Rainbows

Who am I now?
How do I contribute?
What can I do
to make a difference here?
With what I am,
What I have been given?

My words matter.
The are what only I can do.
My stories fall like stones into water
Causing ripples that change
who we are together.

Let my words matter.
Let my words become concrete
—ink on the page.
Let my words make money.
Be the product of my self that pays the bills

Changes the face of our lives
Becomes the gift that I give.

Help me not hide my light under a bushel,
    My words in a drawer,
    Instead, help me choose to give them
    to the world
    A tiny candle flickering
    in the shelter of my hand
    Protected from the harsh winds.

Help me shine with love
    Make rainbows through the broken
    Become not the answer
    But the gift of question.
    Help me do the one small thing can I do now
    That moves my world closer
    To where I am called to be.
    Let me become laughing curiosity
    Kind effort
    Caring and practiced love
    Consistent hands on keyboard
    Deep joy in the face of the broken.

Help me act, move, experience
    Not regret the time I have spent.
    Let me bask in the sunshine
    And dance in the rain.
    Rains come and go
    And sunshine gives way to night.
    Beauty, love, hope, shine through both.
    Light shines through the broken, makes
    Rainbows of reflection

Through the cracks of our lives.

I AM ONE VOICE
  Writing in the wilderness.
  One tiny candle, one weak flame,
  Lit in the dark.
  One hope that believes
  Love is more powerful that black and white.
  Truth is more powerful than wealth.
  And Hope will change the world.
  Wild Joy leading to words
  Bringing light that makes
  Rainbows through broken glass.

Lighthouse

You are the Lighthouse
Shining in the darkness.
Light, love,
for someone else to cling to.
Be present.
Be real.
Do your work.
Sit in a chair,
Write your words.
Then reach out.
Let go of the words
Into the world,
Butterflies of light,
Hope, despair, anger,
Change.
Greet the dawn Tomorrow,
Rise and fall with the moon.
Type your laughter, your joy,
Your anger, your sorrow, Your tears,
And then

Find peace in the nothingness
The spaces between the lines.
The few moments of calm.
Be where you are.
Love deeply
Because in the end
It is your love
And your words
That become the light,
The Butterflies
That change the world.

Hope of the World

Become part of the whole in a different
        But meaningful way.
        Focus. Move forward.
    Live in love and hope.
    Become Centred, calm, focused, joyful.
    Living big picture to small focus.
    Write in love and joy and hope

WALK A LIFE OF MEANING.
    Meaning in the open
    In the face of the broken.
    Meaning in the building of laughter
    In the process of change
    In becoming.

MOVE ONE HABIT AT A TIME
    Towards the person you wish to become.
    Own your choices.

Own your life
This collection of results
Of a million tiny choices.
Walk in it, head high,
Becoming,
Knowing that changes comes
In the smallest pice of different choices,
The smallest hope
The smallest step off the beaten path.

THERE IS SOMETHING THERE
Outside yourself
Outside this mind numbing
Overwhelming chaos
That calls you forward,
Calls you into the meadow of green
Beyond the valley of shadows.
It holds you deep and hard.
It will not let you fall.

STEP INTO THAT LIGHT,
Crawl if you must.
You are called, broken and whole,
As you are.
Given the message to speak,
To write
To share.
Take joy in that gift
And courage too.
Deep breaths that reframe your fear
As joyful anticipation and excitement
That helps you step out of the shadows
And holds up the light of your gift to the world.

· · ·

WORDS UPON THE PAGE
Are so much more than black and white.
The are hope.
They are dreams and change
To a seeking world.

Acknowledgments

Many people helped me along with path that was recovery and poem to book. Thanks go:

To my husband Lloyd, who believes in me even when I struggle to believe in myself, who edits out my extra commas and listens to me read everything aloud, I cannot tell you how much your support has meant over the years we have been together.

To my children, Nicole and Patricia, who have listened to my first drafts, second drafts, third drafts, fourth drafts, and always cheered me on, made tea, ordered pizza, and plotted world domination (aka book marketing). You are the best!

To the Many Health Professionals who Helped me Recover: My team at Altum Health, the assessment team at the Toronto Rehabilitation Institute, and my personal health team, particularly Dr. Sue, who kept reminding me to be present and do the work. I would not be where I am today without your help.

To the many writers who fill my life particularly Cindy and

THE MEMBERS OF THE GWN, the Accountability group and the Wednesday Night Write In (Kat, Amy, Pam, John, Patch, Jess, Evan, and so many more over the years). You have each inspired me, kept me on track, and encouraged me repeatedly to let you all read what I wrote. Your support means more than I can ever say in words.

TO THE MEMBERS OF RAVENCLAW ELDER DORM, particularly Sparrow, Daisy and Ielith. Thank you for all the times you encouraged me to just keep going, to keep writing. Thank you for all the times you listened and for sharing your own stories with me. Our friendship has allowed us to grow and become artists, each in our own right, and I am blessed to have each of you in my life.

AND TO YOU, DEAR READER, because without you, these would be just words scribbled in the darkness, stuffed in a drawer. You give them the courage to become butterflies on the winds of life.

About the Author

Eli Winfield writes in a variety of genres, including poetry, suspense, science fiction, high and low fantasy, urban fantasy, and medieval romance. You never know what her muse will give you next.

facebook.com/eli.winfield.author

Also by Eli Winfield

North Watch Keep

Can the King's Hound of Justice, Sir Kelvrin of Alymes, help Lady Beth, the only surviving member of North Watch Keep,and reclaim North Watch from Lord Geoffry of Gwen Myer before it is too late? (Novella, 16K words)

Available on Amazon and Kobo.